IC COOKBOOK

40+ Soup, Pizza, and Side Dishes recipes designed for Interstitial Cystitis diet

TABLE OF CONTENTS

equally by a Committee of the American Bar Association and a Committee of Publishers and Associations.

Introduction

IC recipes for personal enjoyment but also for family enjoyment. You will love them for sure for how easy it is to prepare them.

SOUP RECIPES

ZUCCHINI SOUP

Serves: *4*

Prep Time: *10*   Minutes

Cook Time: *20*   Minutes

Total Time: *30*   Minutes

INGREDIENTS

- 1 tablespoon olive oil
- 1 lb. zucchini
- ¼ red onion
- ½ cup all-purpose flour
- ¼ tsp salt
- ¼ tsp pepper
- 1 can vegetable broth
- 1 cup heavy cream

DIRECTIONS

1. In a saucepan heat olive oil and sauté zucchini until tender
2. Add remaining ingredients to the saucepan and bring to a boil
3. When all the vegetables are tender transfer to a blender and blend until smooth
4. Pour soup into bowls, garnish with parsley and serve

Serves: **4**

Prep Time: **10**   Minutes

Cook Time: **20**   Minutes

Total Time: **30**   Minutes

INGREDIENTS

- 2 tablespoon olive oil
- 2 onons
- 2 garlic clvoes
- ¼ tsp red pepper flakes
- 2 lb. broccoli
- 1 potato

DIRECTIONS

1. In a saucepan heat olive oil and sauté brocoli until tender
2. Add remaining ingredients to the saucepan and bring to a boil
3. When all the vegetables are tender transfer to a blender and blend until smooth
4. Pour soup into bowls, garnish with parsley and serve

SIDE DISHES

FRIED VEGETABLES

Serves: **2**

Prep Time: **10**   Minutes

Cook Time: **15**   Minutes

Total Time: **25**   Minutes

INGREDIENTS

- 1 cup red bell pepper
- ¼ cup cucumber
- ¼ cup zucchini
- ¼ cup asparagus
- ¼ cup carrots
- 1 onion
- 2 eggs
- 1 tsp salt
- 1 tsp pepper
- Seasoning
- 1 tablespoon olive oil

DIRECTIONS

1. In a skillet heat olive oil and sauté onion until soft
2. Chop vegetables into thin slices and pour over onion

3. Whisk eggs with salt and pepper and pour over the vegetables
4. Cook until vegetables are brown
5. When ready remove from heat and serve

Serves: **4**

Prep Time: **10**   Minutes

Cook Time: **55**   Minutes

Total Time: **65**   Minutes

INGREDIENTS

- 1 onion
- 2 garlic cloves
- ¼ lb. carrots
- 1 potato
- 1 tablespoon balsamic vinegar
- ¼ tsp salt
- ¼ tsp black pepper
- 1 tablespoon olive oil
- 1 cup water

DIRECTIONS

1. Chop all the vegetables and place them in a heated skillet
2. Add remaining ingredients and cook on low heat
3. Allow to simmer for 40-45 minutes or until vegetables are soft
4. Transfer mixture to a blender and blend until smooth
5. When ready remove from the blender and serve

FISH "CAKE"

Serves: *4-6*
Prep Time: *10*   Minutes

Cook Time: *50*   Minutes

Total Time: *60*   Minutes

INGREDIENTS

- 2 tuna tins
- 2 potatoes
- 2 eggs
- 1 handful of gluten free flour
- 1 handful of parsley
- black pepper
- 1 cup breadcrumbs

DIRECTIONS

1. Preheat the oven to 350 F
2. Boil the potatoes until they are soft
3. Mix the tuna with parsley, black pepper and salt
4. Roll fish into patties and dip into a bowl with flour, then eggs and then breadcrumbs
5. Place the patties on a baking tray
6. Bake at 350 F for 40-45 minutes
7. When ready remove from heat and serve

SUSHI HANDROLLS

Serves: **2**

Prep Time: **10** Minutes

Cook Time: **25** Minutes

Total Time: **35** Minutes

INGREDIENTS

- 1 sushi nori packet
- 4 tablespoons mayonnaise
- ½ lb. smoked salmon
- 1 tsp wasabi
- 1 cup cooked sushi rice
- 1 avocado

DIRECTIONS

1. Cut avocado and into thin slices
2. Take a sheet of sushi and spread mayonnaise onto the sheet
3. Add rice, salmon and avocado
4. Roll and dip sushi into wasabi and serve

STEAMED VEGETABLES

Serves: **2**

Prep Time: **10**   Minutes

Cook Time: **10**   Minutes

Total Time: **20**   Minutes

INGREDIENTS

- 1 carrot
- 2 sweet potato
- 2 parsnips
- 1 zucchini
- 2 broccoli stems

DIRECTIONS

1. Chop vegetables into thin slices
2. Place all the vegetables into a steamer
3. Add enough water and cook on high until vegetables are steamed
4. When ready remove from the steamer and serve

GUACAMOLE

Serves: **2**

Prep Time: **5** Minutes

Cook Time: **5** Minutes

Total Time: **10** Minutes

INGREDIENTS

- 1 avocado
- 1 lime juice
- 1 handful of coriander
- 1 tsp olive oil
- 1 tsp salt
- 1 tsp pepper

DIRECTIONS

1. **Place all the ingredients in a blender**
2. **Blend until smooth and transfer to a bowl**

Serves:	**4-6**
Prep Time:	**15** Minutes
Cook Time:	**35** Minutes
Total Time:	**50** Minutes

INGREDIENTS

- 2 chicken breasts
- Tortilla chips
- Fajita seasoning
- ¼ cup cheddar cheese
- 4-5 mushrooms
- Guacamole
- ¼ cup peppers

DIRECTIONS

1. In a pan heat olive oil and add chopped onion, sauté until soft
2. Add chicken, fajita seasoning and remaining vegetables
3. Cook on low heat for 10-12 minutes
4. Place tortilla chips into a baking dish, sprinkle cheese and bake in the oven until cheese has melted
5. Remove from the oven pour sautéed vegetables and chicken over and tortilla chips and serve

SCRAMBLED EGGS WITH SALMON

Serves: **2**

Prep Time: **10** Minutes

Cook Time: **20** Minutes

Total Time: **30** Minutes

INGREDIENTS

- ½ lb. smoked salmon
- 2 eggs
- 1 avocado
- 1 tsp salt
- 1 tsp pepper
- 1 tps olive oil

DIRECTIONS

1. In a bowl whisk the eggs with salt and pepper
2. In a skillet heat olive oil and pour the egg mixture
3. Add salmon pieces to the mixture and cook for 2-3 minutes per side
4. When ready remove from the skillet, add avocado and serve

Serves: **4**

Prep Time: **10** Minutes

Cook Time: **25** Minutes

Total Time: **35** Minutes

INGREDIENTS

- 2 chicken breasts
- 1 cup cooked white rice
- 2 tablespoons mayonnaise
- 1 tablespoon curry powder
- 1 zucchini
- 1 cup broccoli
- 1 tablespoon olive oil

DIRECTIONS

1. Cut chicken breast into small pieces and set aside
2. In a pan heat olive oil and cook the chicken breast for 4-5 minutes
3. In another bowl combine mayonnaise, curry powder and add mixture to the chicken
4. Add remaining ingredients and cook for another 10-12 minutes or until the chicken is ready
5. When ready remove from the pot and serve with white rice

ROASTED VEGETABLES

Serves: **2**

Prep Time: **10** Minutes

Cook Time: **50** Minutes

Total Time: **60** Minutes

INGREDIENTS

- 1 carrot
- 2 sweet potatoes
- 1 butternut squash
- 2 parsnips
- 1 rosemary spring
- 2 bay leaves

DIRECTIONS

1. Chop the vegetables into thin slices
2. Place everything in a prepare baking dish
3. Bake at 350 F for 40-45 minutes or until vegetables are golden brown
4. When ready remove from the oven and serve

Serves: *1*
Prep Time: 5   Minutes

Cook Time: 5   Minutes

Total Time: *10*   Minutes

INGREDIENTS

- 1 cabbage
- 1 bunch of baby carrots
- ½ cucumber
- 1 bun of cilantro
- 1 bunch of basil
- 1 onion

DIRECTIONS

1. **In a bowl mix all ingredients and mix well**
2. **Serve with dressing**

Serves: *1*
Prep Time: 5   Minutes

Cook Time: 5   Minutes

Total Time: *10*   Minutes

INGREDIENTS

- 1 egg
- ¼ cup rice vinegar
- 1 tablespoon coconut aminos
- 1 tablespoon sriracha
- 1 tablespoon maple syrup

DIRECTIONS

1. In a bowl mix all ingredients and mix well
2. Serve with dressing

Serves: **1**

Prep Time: 5   Minutes

Cook Time: 5   Minutes

Total Time: **10**   Minutes

INGREDIENTS

- 2 cups arugula leaves
- ¼ cup cranberries
- ¼ cup honey
- ¼ cup pecans
- 1 cup salad dressing

DIRECTIONS

1. In a bowl mix all ingredients and mix well
2. Serve with dressing

MASOOR SALAD

Serves: *1*

Prep Time: *5*   Minutes

Cook Time: *5*   Minutes

Total Time: *10*   Minutes

INGREDIENTS

- ¼ cup masoor
- ¼ cup cucumber
- ½ cup carrot
- ¼ cup tomatoes
- ¼ cup onion

SALAD DRESSING

- ¼ tablespoon olive oil
- 1 tsp lemon juice
- ¼ tsp green chillies
- ½ tsp black pepper

DIRECTIONS

1. In a bowl combine all ingredients together
2. Add salad dressing, toss well and serve

Serves: *1*
Prep Time: 5   Minutes

Cook Time: 5   Minutes

Total Time: *10*   Minutes

INGREDIENTS

- 1 cup muskmelon
- ½ cup pear cubes
- ½ cup apple cubes
- Salad dressing

DIRECTIONS

1. In a bowl combine all ingredients together
2. Add salad dressing, toss well and serve

Serves: **1**

Prep Time: **5** Minutes

Cook Time: **5** Minutes

Total Time: **10** Minutes

INGREDIENTS

- 2 cups watermelon
- ¼ cup orange
- ¼ cup sweet lime
- ¼ cup pomegranate

SALAD DRESSING
- 1 tsp olive oil
- 1 tsp lemon juice
- 1 tablespoon parsley

DIRECTIONS

1. In a bowl combine all ingredients together
2. Add salad dressing, toss well and serve

POTATO SALAD

Serves: **2**

Prep Time: **5**   Minutes

Cook Time: **10**   Minutes

Total Time: **15**   Minutes

INGREDIENTS

- 5 potatoes
- 1 tsp cumin seeds
- 1/3 cup oil
- 2 tsp mustard
- 1 red onion
- 2 cloves garlic
- 1/3 cup lemon juice
- 1 tsp sea salt

DIRECTIONS

1. Steam the potatoes until tender
2. Mix mustard, turmeric powder, lemon juice, cumin seeds, and salt
3. Place the potatoes in a bowl and pour the lemon mixture over
4. Add the chopped onion and minced garlic over
5. Stir to coat and refrigerate covered
6. Add oil and stir before serving

Serves: **2**

Prep Time: **5**   Minutes

Cook Time: **5**   Minutes

Total Time: **10**   Minutes

INGREDIENTS

- 1 ½ tbs lemon juice
- 1/3 tsp salt
- ¼ tsp black pepper
- 2 tbs olive oil
- 1/3 lb carrots
- 1 tsp mustard

DIRECTIONS

1. Mix mustard, lemon juice and oil together
2. Peel and shred the carrots in a bowl
3. Stir in the dressing and season with salt and pepper
4. Mix well and allow to chill for at least 30 minutes

MOROCCAN SALAD

Serves: **2**

Prep Time: **5**   Minutes

Cook Time: **5**   Minutes

Total Time: **10**   Minutes

INGREDIENTS

- 2 tbs lemon juice
- 1 tsp cumin
- 1 tsp paprika
- 3 tbs olive oil
- 2 cloves garlic
- 5 carrots
- Salt
- Pepper

DIRECTIONS

1. Peel and slice the carrots
2. Add the carrots in boiled water and simmer for at least 5 minutes
3. Drain and rinse the carrots under cold water
4. Add in a bowl
5. Mix the lemon juice, garlic, cumin, paprika, and olive oil together

6. Pour the mixture over the carrots and toss then season with salt and pepper
7. Serve immediately

AVOCADO CHICKEN SALAD

Serves: **2**

Prep Time: **5**   Minutes

Cook Time: **5**   Minutes

Total Time: **10**   Minutes

INGREDIENTS

- 3 tsp lime juice
- 3 tbs cilantro
- 1 chicken breast
- 1 avocado
- 1/3 cup onion
- 1 apple
- 1 cup celery
- Salt
- Pepper
- Olive oil

DIRECTIONS

1. Dice the chicken breast
2. Season with salt and pepper and cook into a greased skillet until golden
3. Dice the vegetables and place over the chicken in a bowl
4. Mash the avocado and sprinkle in the cilantro

5. Season with salt and pepper and add lime juice
6. Serve drizzled with olive oil

ASPARAGUS FRITATTA

Serves: **2**

Prep Time: **10**   Minutes

Cook Time: **20**   Minutes

Total Time: **30**   Minutes

INGREDIENTS

- ½ lb. asparagus
- 1 tablespoon olive oil
- ½ red onion
- ¼ tsp salt
- 2 oz. cheddar cheese
- 1 garlic clove
- ¼ tsp dill

DIRECTIONS

1. In a bowl whisk eggs with salt and cheese
2. In a frying pan heat olive oil and pour egg mixture
3. Add remaining ingredients and mix well
4. Serve when ready

EGGPLANT FRITATTA

Serves: **2**

Prep Time: **10** Minutes

Cook Time: **20** Minutes

Total Time: **30** Minutes

INGREDIENTS

- ½ lb. eggplant
- 1 tablespoon olive oil
- ½ red onion
- ¼ tsp salt
- 2 oz. cheddar cheese
- 1 garlic clove
- ¼ tsp dill

DIRECTIONS

1. In a bowl whisk eggs with salt and cheese
2. In a frying pan heat olive oil and pour egg mixture
3. Add remaining ingredients and mix well
4. Serve when ready

KALE FRITATTA

Serves: **2**

Prep Time: **10** Minutes

Cook Time: **20** Minutes

Total Time: **30** Minutes

INGREDIENTS

- ½ lb. kale
- 1 tablespoon olive oil
- ½ red onion
- ¼ tsp salt
- 2 oz. parmesan cheese
- 1 garlic clove
- ¼ tsp dill

DIRECTIONS

1. In a bowl whisk eggs with salt and parmesan cheese
2. In a frying pan heat olive oil and pour egg mixture
3. Add remaining ingredients and mix well
4. Serve when ready

Serves: **2**

Prep Time: **10**   Minutes

Cook Time: **20**   Minutes

Total Time: **30**   Minutes

INGREDIENTS

- 1 cup broccoli
- 1 tablespoon olive oil
- ½ red onion
- ¼ tsp salt
- 2 oz. cheddar cheese
- 1 garlic clove
- ¼ tsp dill

DIRECTIONS

1. In a skillet sauté broccoli until tender
2. In a bowl whisk eggs with salt and cheese
3. In a frying pan heat olive oil and pour egg mixture
4. Add remaining ingredients and mix well
5. When ready serve with sautéed broccoli

STUFFED SWEET POTATOES

Serves: **4**

Prep Time: **10** Minutes

Cook Time: **20** Minutes

Total Time: **30** Minutes

INGREDIENTS

- 2 lbs sweet potatoes
- 1 avocado
- 1/3 cup cilantro
- 1 jalapeno
- 2 tbs olive oil
- 1 cup black beans
- 1 red onion
- 2 garlic cloves
- 1 cup corn
- 1 cup tomatoes
- 2 tbs taco seasoning
- ½ tsp salt

DIRECTIONS

1. Cook the sweet potatoes as you desire
2. Sauté the jalapeno and red onion in olive oil for 3 minutes

3. Add minced garlic and cook for 1 more minute
4. Add the black beans, corn, seasoning, salt, and pepper and cook 5 more minutes
5. Scoop out the potato insides and fill with the mixture
6. Serve with sour cream

CHICKEN AND RICE

Serves: **4**

Prep Time: **10**   Minutes

Cook Time: **20**   Minutes

Total Time: **30**   Minutes

INGREDIENTS

- 1 cup rice
- 3 tsp seasoning
- 4 chicken breasts
- 2 ½ tbs butter
- 2 ½ cup chicken broth
- 1 lemon
- Salt
- Pepper

DIRECTIONS

1. Season the chicken with salt, pepper and seasoning
2. Cook in melted butter until golden on both sides
3. Add in chicken broth, rice, lemon juice and remaining seasoning
4. Cook covered for at least 20 minutes

LIVER AND MASHED VEGETABLES

Serves: **4**

Prep Time: **20**   Minutes

Cook Time: **40**   Minutes

Total Time: **60**   Minutes

INGREDIENTS

- 3 tsp rapeseed oil
- 350g sweet potato
- 150g parsnip
- 320g green beans
- 350g swede
- 3 cloves garlic
- 15 g flour
- 4 onions
- 1 pack liver
- 1 cube lamb stock
- Black pepper

DIRECTIONS

1. Cook the onions in hot oil for about 20 minutes
2. Coat the liver with flour and pepper and cook in a pan until brown
3. Add the garlic to the onions and stir in 2 tsp of flour

4. Dissolve the stock cube in 450 ml water, then pour over the onions and bring to a boil

5. Add the liver and cook for 5 more minutes

6. Boil the vegetables covered for about 15 minutes

7. Mash the potato, parsnip and swede together

8. Serve the liver with the mashed vegetables

BROCCOLI CASSEROLE

Serves: **4**

Prep Time: **10**   Minutes

Cook Time: **15**   Minutes

Total Time: **25**   Minutes

INGREDIENTS

- 1 onion
- 2 chicken breasts
- 2 tablespoons unsalted butter
- 2 eggs
- 2 cups cooked rice
- 2 cups cheese
- 1 cup parmesan cheese
- 2 cups cooked broccoli

DIRECTIONS

1. Sauté the veggies and set aside
2. Preheat the oven to 425 F
3. Transfer the sautéed veggies to a baking dish, add remaining ingredients to the baking dish
4. Mix well, add seasoning and place the dish in the oven
5. Bake for 12-15 minutes or until slightly brown
6. When ready remove from the oven and serve

ROASTED SQUASH

Serves: *3-4*

Prep Time: *10*   Minutes

Cook Time: *20*   Minutes

Total Time: *30*   Minutes

INGREDIENTS

- 2 delicata squashes
- 2 tablespoons olive oil
- 1 tsp curry powder
- 1 tsp salt

DIRECTIONS

1. Preheat the oven to 400 F
2. Cut everything in half lengthwise
3. Toss everything with olive oil and place onto a prepared baking sheet
4. Roast for 18-20 minutes at 400 F or until golden brown
5. When ready remove from the oven and serve

ZUCCHINI CHIPS

Serves: **2**

Prep Time: **10**   Minutes

Cook Time: **20**   Minutes

Total Time: **30**   Minutes

INGREDIENTS

- 1 lb. zucchini
- 1 tablespoon salt
- 1 tsp smoked paprika

DIRECTIONS

1. Preheat the oven to 425 F
2. In a bowl toss everything with olive oil and seasoning
3. Spread everything onto a prepared baking sheet
4. Bake for 8-10 minutes or until crisp
5. When ready remove from the oven and serve

Serves: **2**

Prep Time: **10**   Minutes

Cook Time: **20**   Minutes

Total Time: **30**   Minutes

INGREDIENTS

- 1 lb. zucchini
- 1 tablespoon salt
- 1 tsp smoked paprika

DIRECTIONS

6. Preheat the oven to 425 F
7. In a bowl toss everything with olive oil and seasoning
8. Spread everything onto a prepared baking sheet
9. Bake for 8-10 minutes or until crisp
10. When ready remove from the oven and serve

PIZZA

ZUCCHINI PIZZA

Serves: *6-8*

Prep Time: *10*   Minutes

Cook Time: *15*   Minutes

Total Time: *25*   Minutes

INGREDIENTS

- 1 pizza crust
- ½ cup tomato sauce
- ¼ black pepper
- 1 cup zucchini slices
- 1 cup mozzarella cheese
- 1 cup olives

DIRECTIONS

1. Spread tomato sauce on the pizza crust
2. Place all the toppings on the pizza crust
3. Bake the pizza at 425 F for 12-15 minutes
4. When ready remove pizza from the oven and serve

Serves: **6-8**

Prep Time: **10**   Minutes

Cook Time: **15**   Minutes

Total Time: **25**   Minutes

INGREDIENTS

- 1 pizza crust
- 8 oz. ricotta cheese
- 1 clove garlic
- 2 oz. parmesan cheese
- ½ lb. baby leaf greens
- 1 tablespoon olive oil

DIRECTIONS

1. Spread tomato sauce on the pizza crust
2. Place all the toppings on the pizza crust
3. Bake the pizza at 425 F for 12-15 minutes
4. When ready remove pizza from the oven and serve

SALMON PIZZA

Serves:	*6-8*
Prep Time:	*10* Minutes
Cook Time:	*15* Minutes
Total Time:	*25* Minutes

INGREDIENTS

- 1 pizza crust
- 1 shallot
- 1 parmesan cheese
- ½ red onion
- 2 tablespoons olive oil
- ½ lb. smoked salmon
- ½ lemon

DIRECTIONS

1. Spread tomato sauce on the pizza crust
2. Place all the toppings on the pizza crust
3. Bake the pizza at 425 F for 12-15 minutes
4. When ready remove pizza from the oven and serve

Serves: **6-8**

Prep Time: **10**   Minutes

Cook Time: **15**   Minutes

Total Time: **25**   Minutes

INGREDIENTS

- 1 onion
- 1 pizza crust
- 1 cup green olives
- 1 clove garlic
- ½ lb. potatoes
- ½ lb. taleggio

DIRECTIONS

1. Spread tomato sauce on the pizza crust
2. Place all the toppings on the pizza crust
3. Bake the pizza at 425 F for 12-15 minutes
4. When ready remove pizza from the oven and serve

CAULIFLOWER PIZZA

Serves: **6-8**

Prep Time: **10**   Minutes

Cook Time: **15**   Minutes

Total Time: **25**   Minutes

INGREDIENTS

- 1 pizza crust
- 2 oz. parmesan cheese
- 1 tablespoon olive oil
- 4-5 basil leaves
- 1 cup mozzarella cheese
- 1 cup cauliflower

DIRECTIONS

1. Spread tomato sauce on the pizza crust
2. Place all the toppings on the pizza crust
3. Bake the pizza at 425 F for 12-15 minutes
4. When ready remove pizza from the oven and serve

ARTICHOKE AND SPINACH PIZZA

Serves: *6-8*

Prep Time: *10*   Minutes

Cook Time: *15*   Minutes

Total Time: *25*   Minutes

INGREDIENTS

- 1 pizza crust
- 1 garlic clove
- ½ lb. spinach
- ½ lb. soft cheese
- 2 oz. artichoke hearts
- 1 cup mozzarella cheese
- 1 tablespoon olive oil

DIRECTIONS

1. Spread tomato sauce on the pizza crust
2. Place all the toppings on the pizza crust
3. Bake the pizza at 425 F for 12-15 minutes
4. When ready remove pizza from the oven and serve

Serves: **6-8**
Prep Time: **10** Minutes

Cook Time: **15** Minutes

Total Time: **25** Minutes

INGREDIENTS

- 1 pizza crust
- 1 olive oil
- 1 garlic clove
- 1 cup mozzarella cheese
- 2 oz. mint
- 2 courgettes

DIRECTIONS

1. Spread tomato sauce on the pizza crust
2. Place all the toppings on the pizza crust
3. Bake the pizza at 425 F for 12-15 minutes
4. When ready remove pizza from the oven and serve

SAUSAGE PIZZA

Serves: *6-8*

Prep Time: *10*   Minutes

Cook Time: *15*   Minutes

Total Time: *25*   Minutes

INGREDIENTS

- 2 pork sausages
- 1 tablespoon olive oil
- 2 garlic cloves
- 1 tsp fennel seeds
- ½ lb. ricotta
- 1 cup mozzarella cheese
- 1 oz. parmesan cheese
- 1 pizza crust

DIRECTIONS

1. Spread tomato sauce on the pizza crust
2. Place all the toppings on the pizza crust
3. Bake the pizza at 425 F for 12-15 minutes
4. When ready remove pizza from the oven and serve

Serves: **6-8**
Prep Time: **10**   Minutes

Cook Time: **15**   Minutes

Total Time: **25**   Minutes

INGREDIENTS

- 1 pizza crust
- 1 tablespoon olive oil
- 1 garlic clove
- 1 cup tomatoes
- 1 cup mozzarella cheese
- 1 carrot
- 1 cucumber

DIRECTIONS

1. Spread tomato sauce on the pizza crust
2. Place all the toppings on the pizza crust
3. Bake the pizza at 425 F for 12-15 minutes
4. When ready remove pizza from the oven and serve

THANK YOU FOR READING THIS BOOK!

CPSIA information can be obtained
at www.ICGtesting.com
Printed in the USA
BVHW071030040321
601713BV00007B/877

ISBN 978-1-6640-0964-6

90000